PLEASE PASS UP

THE SALT

BY LUCY M. WILLIAMS

For The Children Of
St. Mark's —
Best Regards,
Lucy M. Williams
4-20-95

SANDRIDGE PUBLISHING   1995   INDIANA

Art Direction by Thom Head
Layout Design by Greg Walters
Consulting by Robyn Carmen

Sandridge Publishing
715 Moss Creek Drive, Bloomington, IN 47401
First Edition
Printed in Hong Kong.

Publisher's Cataloging in Publication
(Prepared by Quality Books Inc.)

Williams, Lucy M.
      Please pass up the salt / by Lucy M. Williams ; illustrated by
Tom C. Williams.
      p. cm. -- (Red apple zoo series ; 1)
      Preassigned LCCN: 94-92294.
      ISBN 0-945080-18-2

      1. Nutrition--Children's fiction. 2. Salt--Children's fiction.
3. Nutrition--Fiction. 4. Salt--Fiction.   I. Williams, Tom C.,
ill. II. Title.

PZ7.W555Plea 1995   [E]
                              QBI94-1731

To Alyse and Erin with love – L.W.

To Arleen with love – T.W.

Congo lived at the Red Apple Zoo in a special place for elephants. He and his mother had their own stone house and cool pond, with trees outside their wall.

Congo liked to look at himself in the surface of the pond. He had a beautiful long trunk. He was just beginning to grow two white tusks. And he had funny, wrinkled knees—just like his mamma.

One Saturday morning Congo waited by his wall for the children to stop by.

"Hey, Congo!" Jeff called. He dropped a handful of peanuts inside the wall.

Snortle! Snuffle! Congo picked them up with his trunk one by one and ate them all.

Congo's mother draped her big trunk across his back.

"Come eat your hay, Congo," she said in elephant language.

"It's not good to eat too many salty foods."

"Why not?" asked Congo.

"Because. . . your tusks could turn green. Warts could grow on your trunk," she said. "Why, even your tail could fall off if you eat too much salt."

"You're just teasing," said Congo. "Everyone eats salt."

"Congo! Catch this!" said Tim. He whizzed by on his roller blades and threw a big, salty pretzel over Congo's wall.

Glunk! Congo swallowed it whole.

Erin watched from the bench near Cathy's popcorn cart.
"Can't you boys read?" she pointed to a sign on the lawn.
"It says, 'PLEASE DON'T FEED THE ANIMALS'."

"Don't feed the animals?" Congo stared at the sign. It hadn't been there the day before. "Oh, my life is ruined!" he said. "I love salt."

The children all stopped to look at the sign. "Gee, we don't want to make Congo sick," said Jeff.

"This is awful. This is terrible," said Congo. He raised his trunk. "Ball-ooo!" he bellowed.

Erin looked at him sadly. "Sorry, Congo. It's for your own good." She ate the last handful of popcorn from her bag. "See you later."

All day children and grownups stopped by Congo's place. They all looked at the new sign. No one gave Congo any of their peanuts or popcorn.

"It's a good thing," said his mother.

By the end of the day, when the zoo closed, Congo was so hungry for his salty snacks that he began to stare at the popcorn cart. He stared so hard his eyes crossed. But staring didn't help. He wanted to eat the nice, salty popcorn.

Prices
sm 75¢
med 1.20
Lg 2.40

POPCORN

SALT

"Oh, this is awful! This is terrible!" said Congo.

Then Cathy pushed her cart up under the tree. "See you tomorrow, Congo," she said.

"Well, look at that!" said Congo. Cathy had left her cart very close to the wall. Maybe he could reach the popcorn.

Congo looked one way and he looked the other way. No one walked along the path through the zoo. Everyone had gone home, and his mother had gone into their house.

Only Binka, the tortoise, lay by a rock across the road, and she never noticed anything.

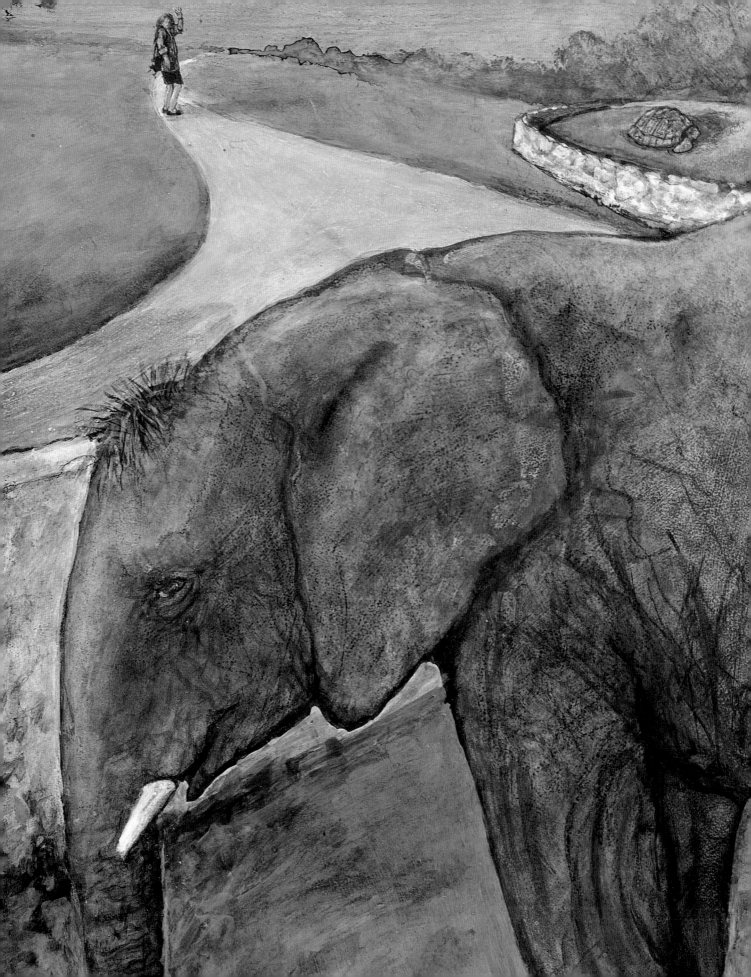

Congo looked at the big mound of salty, yellow popcorn, just waiting to be eaten. . . by an elephant who loved salt.

Congo reached his trunk over the wall. He stretched it as long as he could.

"Ah!" said Congo when he touched the cart at last. "Popcorn! Popcorn! Popcorn! Great mounds of it!"

Congo opened the little glass doors with his trunk and reached in.

Snuffle, snuffle, munchle, crunchle! Congo ate every last kernel, even some that had fallen on the ground.

Oh, it tasted so good. Then Congo picked up the salt shaker and swallowed that, too.

Burrr-urp!

Slowly Congo walked back to his house and lay down in the corner to sleep.

During the night he woke up. "Mamma."

"What's the matter, Congo?" his mother asked sleepily.

"I'm thirsty. I need a drink of water."

"You may go to the pond and get a drink," she answered.

Congo went to the pond. He lowered his trunk into the water and drank. . . and drank. . . and drank. . . and drank.

He was still drinking when the sun came up. By then Congo did not feel well.

"I feel awful! I feel terrible!" he moaned. "Maybe I really did eat too much salt."

He looked into the pond. Only a little water was left in the bottom.

His tusks DID look a little green.

Was that bump on his trunk a WART?

He turned around and looked at his tail. Thank goodness it was still there.

But something else was missing!

Congo looked down. All four of his knees were big and round and shiny. . . not wrinkled, like elephant knees were supposed to be!

"Wahhh! This is awful! This is terrible!" bellowed Congo.

And it was time for the zoo to open again. In fact, Congo could see children rushing down the path to see him.

"Quick! I have to hide," he said. "I can't be seen without my wrinkles." But it was too late.

Erin stopped suddenly. "What's happened to Congo?"

"Yikes!" said Tim. "Congo looks like a big, gray balloon."

"A balloon? Oh, this is worse than awful," said Congo. "Everyone knows balloons pop!"

"Hey, who ate all my popcorn?" asked Cathy.

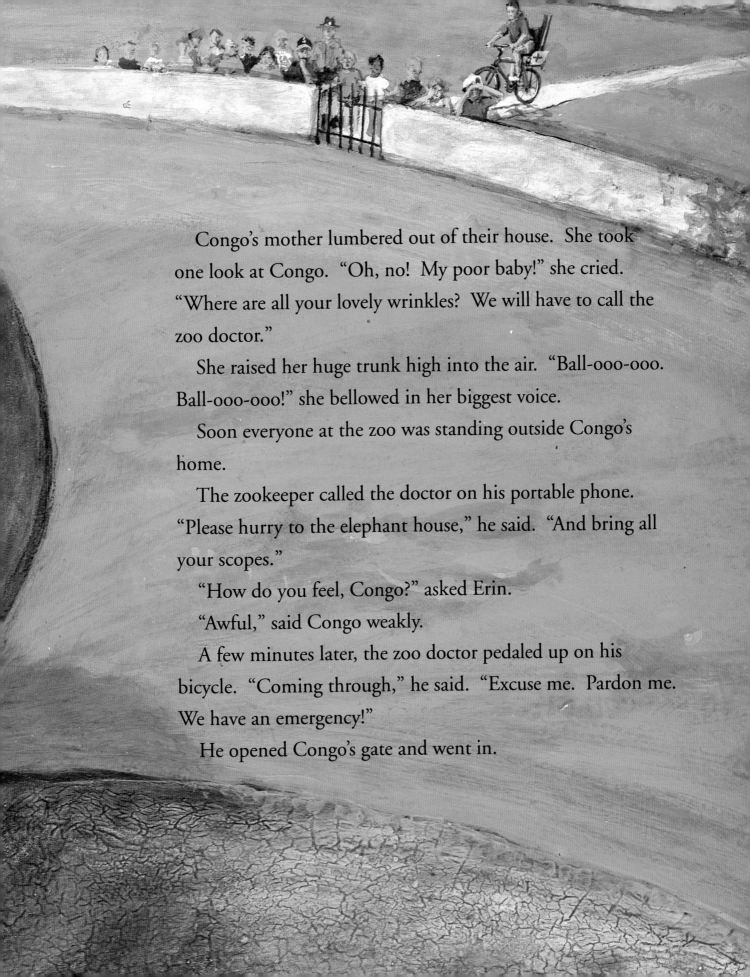

Congo's mother lumbered out of their house. She took one look at Congo. "Oh, no! My poor baby!" she cried. "Where are all your lovely wrinkles? We will have to call the zoo doctor."

She raised her huge trunk high into the air. "Ball-ooo-ooo. Ball-ooo-ooo!" she bellowed in her biggest voice.

Soon everyone at the zoo was standing outside Congo's home.

The zookeeper called the doctor on his portable phone. "Please hurry to the elephant house," he said. "And bring all your scopes."

"How do you feel, Congo?" asked Erin.

"Awful," said Congo weakly.

A few minutes later, the zoo doctor pedaled up on his bicycle. "Coming through," he said. "Excuse me. Pardon me. We have an emergency!"

He opened Congo's gate and went in.

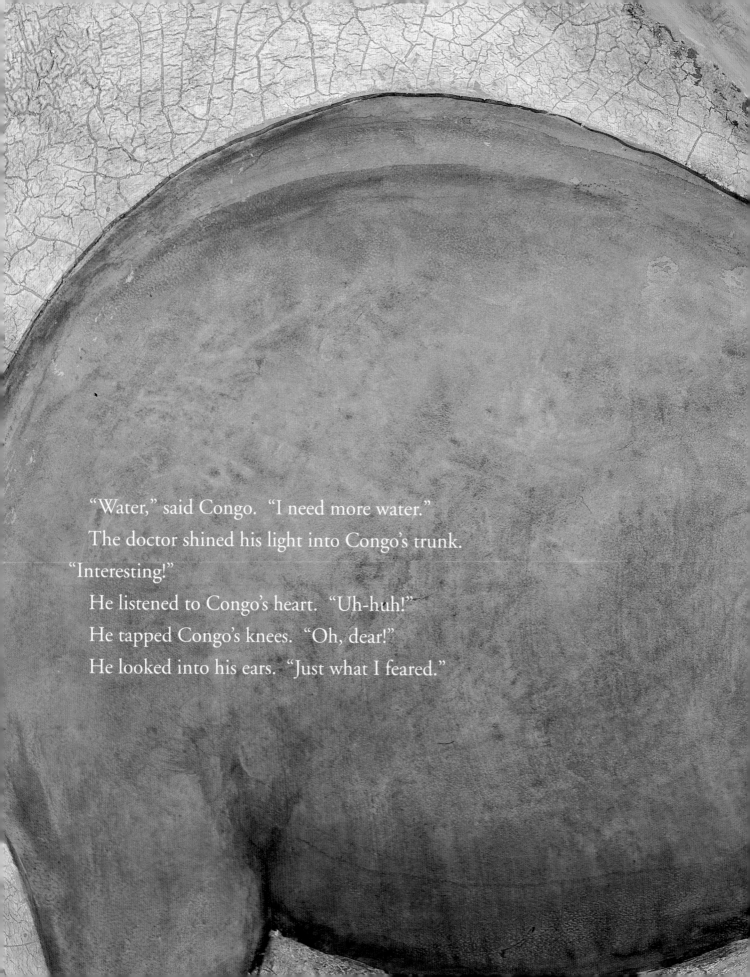

"Water," said Congo. "I need more water."

The doctor shined his light into Congo's trunk. "Interesting!"

He listened to Congo's heart. "Uh-huh!"

He tapped Congo's knees. "Oh, dear!"

He looked into his ears. "Just what I feared."

Everyone waited. The children watched over the wall.
A tear rolled down Erin's cheek.

Congo's mother asked, "What is it, doctor?"

"Well," the doctor said. "I need to do one more test."

Then he stood Congo in front of his fold-up x-ray machine.

"Oh, no!" Cathy said.

There was her salt shaker, still pouring salt into Congo's
stomach.

"Ah-hah!" said the doctor. "Congo's got a very serious
case of . . .

"Salty-osis!"

Everyone gasped.

The other animals came out of their paddocks and started
across the road.

"There must be something we can do," said Jeff.

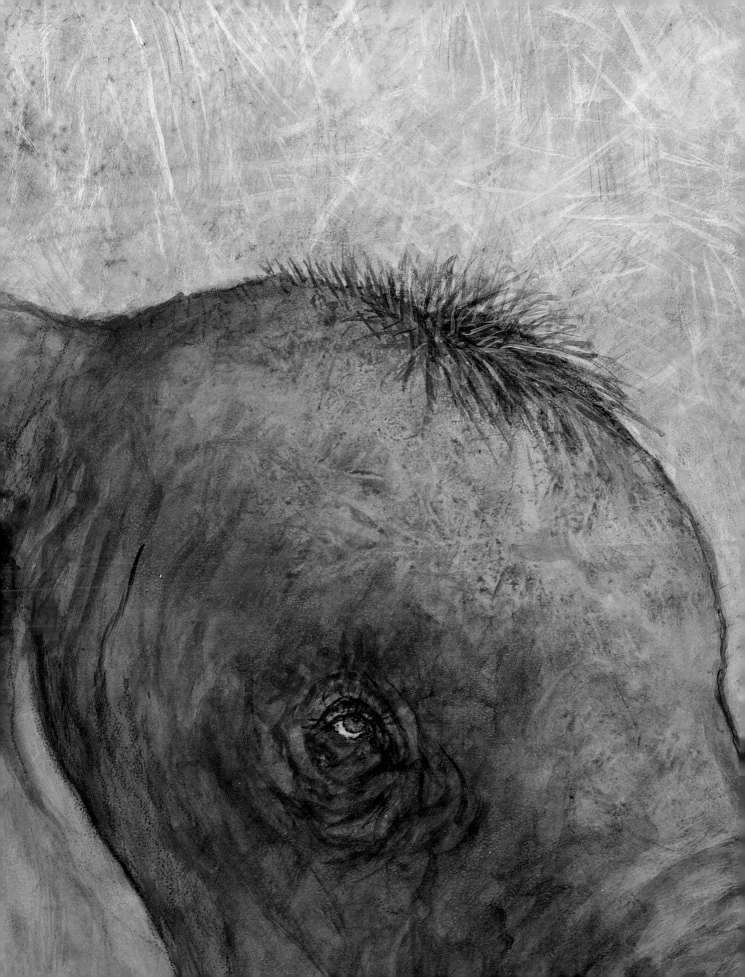

The doctor thought and thought. "Well," he said at last. "I know of only one thing to be done for salty-osis. Congo must eat healthy snacks from now on. No salty peanuts. No salty popcorn. No salty pretzels."

Congo managed to speak. "Nothing but hay?" he asked. "Oooh! I will surely die of food boredom."

"Wrong," said the doctor. "There are lots of healthy foods. Besides, *once in a while* you can eat salty snacks. But you can't eat them all the time. And positively no more salt shakers for you."

"I should hope not," said Cathy.

"Hey, I have an idea," said Erin. "We can take Congo to the market and get him some healthy snacks."

"That's a good idea," said the zookeeper. "I hereby declare a day off at the zoo! Come on, everyone. Let's go help Congo."

So all the gates were opened wide. A great parade headed for the market.

The zookeeper lead the way. Tim followed on his roller blades.

At the door of the supermarket Erin, Jeff, and Tim each got grocery carts.

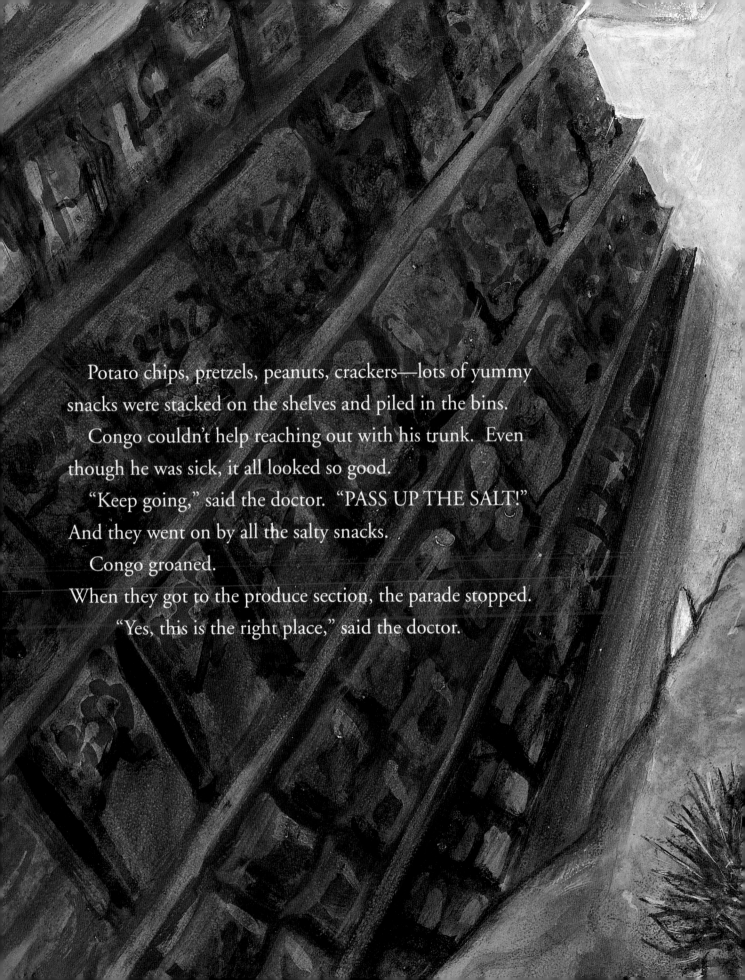

Potato chips, pretzels, peanuts, crackers—lots of yummy snacks were stacked on the shelves and piled in the bins.

Congo couldn't help reaching out with his trunk. Even though he was sick, it all looked so good.

"Keep going," said the doctor. "PASS UP THE SALT!" And they went on by all the salty snacks.

Congo groaned.

When they got to the produce section, the parade stopped.

"Yes, this is the right place," said the doctor.

He filled the carts with juicy oranges, carrots, red grapes, peaches, and lima beans.

"Lima beans!" bellowed Congo.

The doctor put the lima beans back. "Okay, you don't have to eat lima beans," he said. "Now, this way, everyone. We have one more stop."

The doctor led the way up one aisle and down the other. He stopped at aisle seven. He loaded the cart with low salt crackers, unsalted popcorn, and a bag of salt free peanuts.

"Peanuts?" asked Congo, feeling suddenly better. "This isn't awful. It isn't terrible. I can still have some fun snacks. And, I like carrots and peaches and all these healthy foods." He picked some grapes with his trunk and ate them one by one. He could already feel his wrinkles coming back.

"Oh joy! Oh bliss!" said Congo.

Jeff looked in his grocery cart. "Can people eat too much salt?" he asked.

"Yes, indeed," said the doctor. "People need a little bit of salt, but most of us eat way too much."

Cathy said, "Maybe I could sell apples at my cart, along with the popcorn."

"That's a good idea, and I'll put up a new sign," said the zookeeper.

The next morning when Congo and his mother came out of their house, they both looked down at Congo's knees. They were round and gray and. . . wrinkled!

"*All right!*" yelled the children who were waiting by his wall. "Congo is well again."

Congo leaned over the wall to take *just one* peanut from Jeff's hand. He noticed a brand new sign on the lawn.

It said . . .

Why Teach Children About Nutrition

The need for nutrition education for children, even very young children, has become clear. Because of busy schedules and changing roles, parents are not as vigilant as they used to be in providing healthy foods for their kids. And with more and more convenience and "fun" foods on the market, the choices are more difficult than they used to be. This is especially true with snacks that are eaten when parents aren't home.

Obesity, high blood pressure and high blood cholesterol have become problems for children as well as adults in the American population. A healthy diet and a good exercise plan established in childhood can help prevent the development of very real health problems later in life.

Ultimately, it may be up to the children themselves to make healthy choices. A first step, therefore, in teaching kids to make those choices, is to provide them with sound information in a format that is both fun and thought-provoking.

- In "Healthy People 2000," published recently by The Public Health Service of the U.S. Dept. of Health & Human Services, children are identified as an important target group for health promotion and disease prevention initiatives.

- The Secretary of the U.S. Department of Agriculture has announced that school lunches need to be improved by decreasing the amount of salt and fat and increasing the amount of fruits and vegetables served. He also recommended that more effort be expended on nutrition education.

- The current "Dietary Guidelines for Americans," published by the U.S Dept. of Agriculture, advises that any person over two years of age should use salt and sodium only in moderation.

Please Pass Up the Salt is the first of a series of nutrition books that can help parents and teachers educate children about healthier diets.

What We Know About Sodium

- Table salt is composed of two parts—sodium and chloride. It's the sodium that can cause health problems.

- Everyone must have some sodium to live, but most people consume too much. In fact, studies have shown that children consume almost twice the amount of salt needed in one day. A teaspoon of salt contains about 2,000 mg of sodium. Adults and children should limit sodium to 2,400 mg per day, slightly more than 1 teaspoon.

- All foods, even milk, contain some sodium naturally. Extra salt is added as foods are cooked or at the table from the salt shaker. Salt is also added during the processing of foods for enhanced taste and as a preservative. Yet the desire for salt is a learned response. Infants do not naturally like the taste of salt until we add it to their foods and they become accustomed to its taste.

- Sodium attracts water. The more sodium there is in the blood and tissues, the more water there is also. Excess water causes edema—a swelling that occurs especially in the hands, ankles and legs. The extra water also puts pressure on the vessel walls, while forcing the heart to work harder to push the excess water through the body. This high blood pressure increases the risk of stroke, heart attack and kidney failure.

Where to Get More Information About Sodium

American Heart Association, 7320 Greenville Ave., Dallas, TX 75231

U.S. Dept. of Agriculture, Food & Drug Administration, 5600 Fishers Lane, Rockville, MD 20857

Consumer Information Center, Dept. EE, Pueblo, CO 81009

The American Dietetic Association, 216 West Jackson Blvd., Suite 800, Chicago, IL 60606-6995

Suggested Discussion Questions for Children

1. What did Congo the elephant eat that made him so thirsty?

2. Do you think you would really puff up like a balloon if you ate too much salt?

3. Which one of these three foods would taste salty? An orange? Potato chips? A carrot?

4. Name some of your favorite foods. Which ones are salty?

5. On which foods might we shake extra salt? Lemonade? Apples? Mashed potatoes?

6. Taste a lemon, a piece of candy and a salted nut. Can you figure out where on your tongue you taste salty foods?

7. Can you think of ways to eat less salt?

8. Do you salt foods at the table before you taste them?

9. Why is it important to eat less salt?

10. What can you eat for a snack today that is not salty?

Home or Classroom Activities for Children

1. Place a salt shaker in a plastic bag. Add a few drops of water to the bag and close it. Remove the salt shaker a few hours later and notice that it will no longer shake. That's because the salt has absorbed the water. This experiment shows that sodium attracts water, just as it does in our bodies.

2. Open a bag of salted microwave popcorn and notice the surprising amount of salt that is lying in the bottom of the bag.

3. Read some processed food labels. Contents are listed in order of the amount contained in the package. If salt is listed as one of the first few ingredients, the product contains a great deal of salt. Notice how many labels list salt as one of the ingredients.

4. Compare foods that produce the four different taste sensations: salty, sour, bitter and sweet. On which part of the tongue are each of these sensations found?

5. Interview classmates, friends or family members about what foods they like to salt.

6. Using magazine cutouts or food models available from the National Dairy Council, have children guess which foods have the most salt or arrange the foods in order of salt content, with the highest at the top.

7. Let children cut out magazine pictures or draw pictures of favorite snacks. Which snacks are salty?

8. Take a field trip to the grocery story like Congo did or encourage children to be detectives on their own. What kinds of foods should a person buy if their doctor tells them they must eat less salt? Make a list.

9. Collect fast food menus and plan a low salt, fast food meal.

10. Ask children to fold a piece of paper in half and draw pictures of Congo, before and after he ate too much salt.

Sodium Can Be Found in Many Places

1 cup of Campbell's chicken noodle soup = 950 mg
1 cup of Healthy Request chicken noodle soup = 460 mg

1/2 cup plain frozen corn = 6 mg
1/2 cup frozen-in-butter-sauce corn = 310 mg
1/2 cup no-salt-added canned corn = 10 mg
1/2 cup of canned corn = 360 mg

1 cup homemade spaghetti and meatballs = 196 mg
1 cup microwave spaghetti and meatballs = 940 mg
1 cup canned spaghetti and meatballs = 1150 mg

1 ounce Colby or cheddar cheese =190 mg
1 ounce slice of American processed cheese = 340 mg

1 cup plain popped popcorn = 0 mg
1 cup of regular salted microwave popcorn = 100 mg

1 cup milk = 122 mg
Fast food small chocolate milkshake = 300 mg

Fast food hamburger with mustard, no cheese = 241 mg
Fast food cheeseburger = 743 mg

1 slice turkey breast = 29 mg
1 regular beef hotdog = 585 mg

Note - measurements are approximate

Low Salt Spaghetti Sauce

What you need:

1/3 cup chopped onion
2 tablespoons olive oil
1 teaspoon Italian seasoning
27 ounce can (about 3-1/2 cups) no-salt-added tomatoes
6 ounce can no-salt-added tomato paste
8 ounce can no-salt-added tomato sauce
1 teaspoon basil
1 tablespoon minced parsley
1 teaspoon salt
2 teaspoons sugar

How to prepare:

1. In a large saucepan, Sauté the onion in oil slowly until tender
2. Add the remaining ingredients in a large saucepan, cover, simmer over low heat for at least 1 hour. Makes 5 cups.
      Nutrients in 1/2 cup of homemade sauce: 70 calories, 3 grams fat, 222 mg sodium
      Nutrients in 1/2 canned sauce: 96 calories, 4 grams fat, 646 mg sodium

Low Salt Meatballs

What you need:

1/4 cup skim or 1% milk   1 small onion, diced
1-1/2 bread slices   1 egg white
3/4 pound lean ground beef

How to prepare:

1. Combine milk, egg and onion in mixing bowl. Remove crust from bread, crumble and add to mixture. Add meat and mix thoroughly.
2. Shape into 1" balls. Bake on cookie sheet at 375º for 20-30 minutes. Makes about 24 meatballs.
      Nutrients in 4 meatballs: 170 calories, 9 grams fat, 85 mg sodium
      No comparison available

Potato Soup

What you need:

2-1/2 cups cubed potatoes
1 stalk celery, diced
1/3 cup chopped onion
1/4 cup water
1/2 teaspoon salt
1 teaspoon parsley flakes

2 cups skim or 1% milk
4 tablespoons flour
3 tablespoons light margarine

How to prepare:

1. In a 2-quart casserole, combine the potatoes, celery, onion, water and seasonings. Cover.

2. Microwave on HIGH until vegetables are tender, about 8 to 10 minutes. Stir halfw: through the cooking time.

3. Stir 1/4 cup milk with the flour until smooth.

4. Slowly stir flour mixture into remaining milk, margarine and potato mixture.

5. Microwave on HIGH, uncovered, for 8 to 10 minutes until thick. Stir every 2 to 3 minutes. Makes 4 cups.

   Nutrients in 1 cup homemade potato soup: 183 calories, 5 grams fat, 420 mg sodium

   Nutrients in 1 cup canned potato soup: 148 calories, 6.5 grams fat, 1060 mg sodium

Chocolate Pudding

What you need:

- 3 tablespoons unsweetened cocoa
- 1-1/2 tablespoons vegetable oil
- 1/3 cup flour
- 1/3 cup plus 2 tablespoons sugar
- 2-1/2 cups skim or 1% milk
- 3/4 teaspoon vanilla

How to prepare:

1. Combine cocoa, vegetable oil, flour and sugar in a medium saucepan. Mix well.
2. Stir milk SLOWLY into dry ingredients to prevent lumps.
3. Cook over medium heat until mixture thickens. Cool and stir in vanilla. Makes 3 cups.

   Nutrients in 1/2 cup homemade pudding: 156 calories, 4 grams fat, 53 mg sodium

   Nutrients in 1/2 cup boxed instant pudding: 176 calories, 4.5 grams fat, 476 mg sodium